Note to Parents and Teachers

The SCIENCE STARTERS series introduces key science vocabulary and concepts to young children while encouraging them to discover and understand the world around them. The series works as a set of graded readers in three levels.

LEVEL 3: READ ALONE
These books can be read alone or as part of guided or group reading. Each book has three sections:

• Information pages that introduce key concepts. Key words appear in bold for easy recognition on pages where the related science concepts are explained.
• A lively story that recalls this vocabulary and encourages children to use these words when they talk and write.
• A quiz asks children to look back and recall what they have read.

LOOKING AFTER MYSELF looks at HEALTH and DIET. Below are some answers and activities related to the questions on the information spreads that parents, carers, and teachers can use to discuss and develop further ideas and concepts:

p. 6 *What is your body telling you when you feel thirsty?* You need water! A 7-8 year-old should drink around seven glasses of water each day and especially after exercise.

p. 11 *Which muscles feel like they have been working hard after making a bed?*
The arm muscles will probably feel tired, along with back muscles from bending over.

p. 13 *Do you feel your heart and lungs working harder after exercise?* Encourage children to run around playground then feel their faster pulse and breathing. Explain that when we work our body hard our lungs and heart can't keep up so we get out of breath.

p. 17 *Why do you think skin that is hidden under your clothes is paler than the rest of your skin?* Skin hidden from the sun doesn't get tanned like exposed skin.

p. 17 *Why do you need to wear sunglasses when the sun is very bright?* Explain that sunglasses protect our eyes from harmful (UV) rays. Wrap-around sunglasses also protect the tender skin around our eyes.

p. 19 *Why shouldn't you eat food you have dropped on the floor?* The floor is covered in germs that we can't see. Remind children to always wash their hands before eating.

p. 21 *How does rotting fruit look or smell?* If food doesn't look rotten or smell bad, then the taste will often tell us if it is going bad. If in doubt, don't eat it!

p. 23 *Why do you think vacations are important?* Vacations give our bodies a chance to rest. They also allow us to relax and to have fun with family and friends.

ADVISORY TEAM

Educational Consultant
Andrea Bright—Science Coordinator, Trafalgar Junior School

Literacy Consultant
Jackie Holderness—former Senior Lecturer in Primary Education, Westminster Institute, Oxford Brookes University

Series Consultants
Anne Fussell—Early Years Teacher and University Tutor, Westminster Institute, Oxford Brookes University

David Fussell—C.Chem., FRSC

CONTENTS

First published in
the United States in 2006 by
Stargazer Books
c/o The Creative Company
123 South Broad Street
P.O. Box 227, Mankato,
Minnesota 56002

Printed in Malaysia
All rights reserved

Editor: Jim Pipe
Design: Flick, Book Design
and Graphics

Thanks to:
• The pupils of Trafalgar Junior School and
St. Paul's C.E. Primary School for appearing
as models in this book.
• Andrea Bright, Janice Bibby, and Stephanie
Cox for helping to organize the photoshoots.
• The pupils and teachers of Trafalgar Junior
School and St. Nicholas C.E. Infant School
for testing the sample books.

**Library of Congress Cataloging-in-
Publication Data**

Hewitt, Sally.
  Health and diet / by Sally Hewitt.
  p. cm. -- (Science starters. Level 3)
  ISBN 1-59604-011-4
  1. Health--Juvenile literature. 2. Hygiene--
Juvenile literature. 3. Nutrition--Juvenile
literature. 1. Title. II. Series

RA777.H49 2005
613.2--dc22
                      2005046460

Photocredits:
*l-left, r-right, b-bottom, t-top,
c-center, m-middle*
Cover tl, 15mr—Brand X
Pictures. Cover tm & tr, 5br,
7br, 8ml, 14bl, 18br—Corbis.
Cover main, 16tr, 19tl, 22m—
Comstock. 2tr, 2br, 4tl, 9 both,
18tr, 20mr, 22bl, 23—
Iconotec.com. 2mr, 15bl, 23b—
TongRo. 3, 4b, 5tr, 12, 13bl,
16b, 17br, 31tr, 31br—
Photodisc. 5tl, 6ml, 20b—DAJ.
5bl, 11ml, 21br, 31bcr—Jim
Pipe. 6br, 10br, 13tr, 20tl, 24tr,
25 all, 26mr, 27 all, 28-29 all, 30
both, 31ml, 31bcl—Marc
Arundale/ Select Pictures. 7m,
21t—USDA. 8mr, 26ml, 31br—
Stockbyte. 10tl, 14mr, 17tr & m,
22r—Digital Vision. 15t—
Corel. 19mr & bl—PBD. 25bl —
Ingram Publishing.

SCIENCE STARTERS

LEVEL

3

HEALTH AND DIET

Looking After Myself

by Sally Hewitt

Stargazer Books

A HEALTHY BODY

You have an amazing **body**. But you need to look after it so that it stays strong and **healthy**.

Your **body** needs fresh air and exercise, good food, plenty of water, and rest and sleep.

You can help to keep your brain **healthy** by giving yourself lots of interesting things to think about.

Using your brain

Here are some other things that keep
your **body** and brain **healthy**.

Learning
Learning something
new, reading, music,
and playing games are
all good for your brain.

Having fun
Being happy helps to
keep you healthy. Good
friends or a pet to love
can make you feel happy.

Keeping clean
As well as washing your
body, you need to brush
your teeth every day.

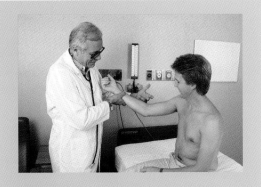

Visiting a doctor
It's good to go to the
doctor and dentist for
a regular check-up.

FOOD AND ENERGY

Every day, your amazing body builds itself and grows. It uses lots of **energy**. It fights germs and heals when you have been hurt.

To be able to do all these things, your body needs **food**.

Using energy

When you feel hungry, your body is telling you it needs food.

What is it telling you when you feel thirsty?

Eat lots of fruit and vegetables.
They are full of vitamins and minerals.

Bread, pasta, and all kinds of cereals give you
energy. These **foods** are called carbohydrates.

A healthy meal

Meat, fish, cheese, and nuts contain proteins. These **foods** help your body to build and grow.

What types of **food** can you see in the meal above?

You need some sugar, salt, and fat every day.

But too many fatty or sweet foods are bad for your health.

LOOKING AFTER YOUR TEETH

Strong **teeth** are important for keeping healthy. You chew your food with them and they give you a nice smile!

Animals that eat meat have pointed **teeth** for tearing. Animals that eat plants have flat **teeth** for chewing.

Pointed teeth

Flat teeth

Look at your teeth in the mirror.

• Find your sharp front teeth, called incisors, for biting.
• Your pointed side teeth, called canines, are for tearing.
• Your flat back teeth, called molars, are for chewing.

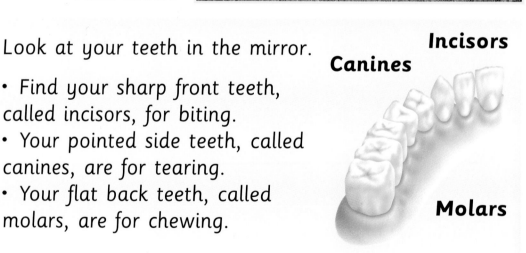

Incisors

Canines

Molars

Look after your **teeth**.
It's hard to eat without them!

Brushing teeth

Brush your **teeth** every morning and
night to get rid of little bits of
food and germs. If they are left
on your **teeth**, they cause tooth decay.

Brush all your **teeth** carefully.
Rinse your mouth out with water.

Tooth decay is when
your teeth go bad.

Too many sweet foods
or drinks can make
your teeth decay.

9

BONES AND MUSCLES

Your body is supported by your skeleton. This is made up of 206 **bones**.

Running, walking, and jumping keep your **bones** strong. The minerals in foods such as fish, nuts, and milk help to build strong **bones** too.

Skeleton

Straight

Slouched

Your posture is how you stand. A straight posture helps your bones to support your body.

Under your skin are about 650 **muscles**. Big **muscles** in your back, legs, and arms pull your bones when you move. **Muscles** inside you work your heart and stomach.

Muscles

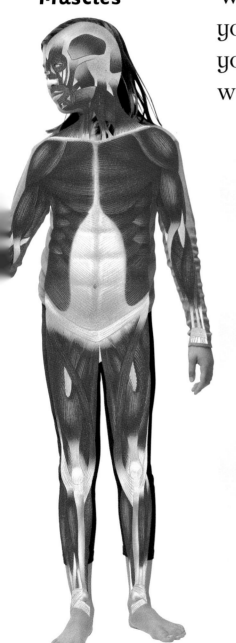

When you move, you work your **muscles**. The harder you make your **muscles** work, the stronger they get.

Make your bed. Fluff up the pillows. Shake out the cover. Tuck in the sheets.

Which muscles feel like they have been working hard?

11

Breathing in

LUNGS AND HEART

Every part of your body needs oxygen from the air. You breathe air through your mouth and down to your **lungs**.

Your **lungs** are like two big sponges. But instead of soaking up water, they soak up air.

Lungs

Sit still. Find your pulse and feel your heartbeat. Put your hand on your chest and feel yourself breathing in and out.

Now do some exercise. Do you feel your heart and lungs working harder?

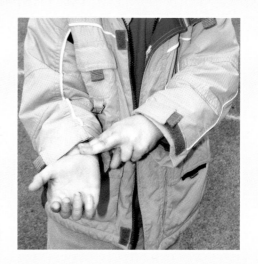

Oxygen from the air goes into your blood. Your **heart** pumps blood full of oxygen around and around your body through tubes called blood vessels.

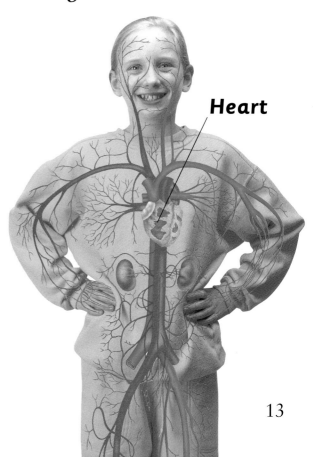

Heart

Running and dancing are the kinds of exercise that work your heart and lungs and keep them healthy.

13

EXERCISE

Exercise makes your body work hard.
It helps to keep you fit and healthy.
You can do all kinds of different **exercise**.

Cycling, skating, and skateboarding
are fun. Wear a helmet, knee
pads, and elbow pads in case
you have a fall!

Skateboarding

You need to
learn how to
cycle safely
on roads and
cycle paths.

Team games

Everyone works hard together in team games.

You train to get fitter and to practice skills. Spectators come to watch you play and cheer when you score!

Walking to school, playing in the park, and making your bed are all kinds of exercise.

What exercise do you do every day? What new exercise would you like to do?

15

SUNSHINE AND FRESH AIR

It feels good to go outside, breathe **fresh air,** and feel the **sunshine** on your skin.

Your skin uses **sunlight** to make vitamin D which helps to make your bones strong. But too much **sun** can burn your skin.

A sunhat and sunscreen can help to protect your skin from the hot sun.

In the sun

Smoke from chimneys, traffic, and cigarettes makes the **air** dirty. It's better not to breathe in too much dirty **air**!

Trees help to keep the **air** clean. The park, the countryside, and the seaside are good places to enjoy the **fresh air**.

Fresh air

Why do you think skin that is hidden under your clothes is paler than the rest of your skin?

Why do you need to wear sunglasses when the sun is very bright?

KEEPING CLEAN

Every day, your hair, skin, and nails get dirty. Your skin gets hot and sweaty.

If you don't wash, the sweat and dirt on your body soon gets smelly.

You need to have a bath or shower, **clean** your nails, and wash your hair to smell **clean**!

Many animals spend lots of time keeping clean.

This rhinoceros is taking a mud bath to clean bugs off its skin!

Paws and feet walk over the floor.

Why shouldn't you eat food you have dropped on the floor?

Washing our skin keeps it healthy. Dirty skin can become sore.

Tiny germs can get into cuts on your skin.

Getting dirty

Your clothes need washing. They get smelly and dirty too!

Germs in dirt on your hands can make you ill.

Wash your hands after you have been to the bathroom and if you have touched soil.

FIGHTING GERMS

Germs that give you coughs and colds fly through the air when you cough and sneeze. Use a hankie so no one else catches them!

Resting and keeping warm when you are sick helps your body to **fight germs** and get better.

Resting

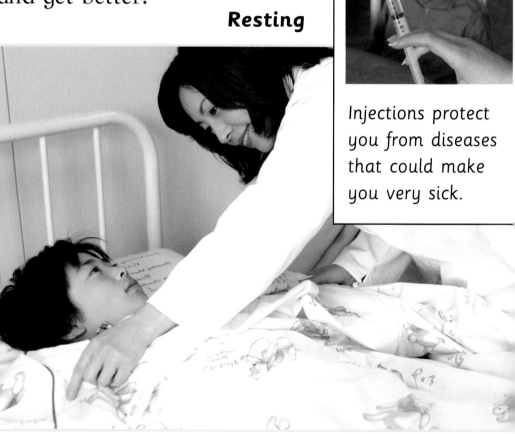

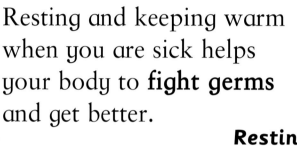

Injections protect you from diseases that could make you very sick.

A clean kitchen

People who prepare food keep the kitchen very clean. They wash their hands before they touch food. A hat holds back their hair.

Fruit and vegetables are washed. Fresh food is stored in a refrigerator.

Germs on food start to make it rot when it gets old.

Our senses can help to warn us. How does rotting fruit look or smell?

Rotting fruit

CHANGE AND REST

Your body works hard all day.
It is important to have a
change and a **rest**.

A drink of water helps your body to work better whatever you are doing.

When you are reading, writing, or working on the computer, take a break and have a good stretch.

Sleeping

Sleep is an important part of keeping healthy. Imagine how tired your body would get if you never went to sleep!

While you are asleep, your body keeps working. Your brain is still thinking, your heart keeps beating, and you keep breathing, but everything slows down.

Weekends and vacations give you a break from school. Why do you think they are important? What activities do you like to do on vacation?

23

I FEEL SICK!

Look for words about your body and keeping healthy.

Mia sneezed very loudly three times. "Oh dear," said Mom. "Have you got a cold?" Mia sneezed again.

"Use your hankie!" said Ronnie. "I don't want to catch your germs."

Mom put Mia to bed. "It's not bedtime!" she cried. But as soon as she curled up under the cover, she fell asleep. Mom and Ronnie tiptoed out of the room.

Mia stayed in bed all the next day. Ronnie started to play a computer game in his bedroom next door.

"Sshh! Not too loud," said Mom. "Mia needs peace and quiet!"

The day after that, Mia felt a bit better.
"I'm bored!" she said.
"I want to go outside
and play!"

"Tomorrow," said Mom.
Mia was very angry and
grouchy. She didn't want
to stay in bed.

Ronnie read Mia a story.
He played cards with her.
He performed a puppet show.

Mia laughed and clapped.

"Thank you for
cheering Mia up,"
Mom said to Ronnie.
"You've helped her
to feel much better."

The next day was warm and sunny.
"You can go outside today," said Mom.
"But first, eat your breakfast."

Mia was hungry.
She had a bowl of
cereal, orange
juice, and a banana.

"That will build
your strength up!"
said Mom.

"I need lots of strength too!" said Ronnie.

"I'm playing in the school
basketball team on Saturday."

After breakfast, they walked
to the park. Mia skipped
with her rope. Ronnie
practiced with his basketball.
Mom threw a ball
for Pluto the dog.

Mom gave them all
a drink of water.
"Don't forget Pluto,"
said Mia.

Mia said, "I'm tired!"
"That's because you've been sick,"
said Mom. "We can come again tomorrow.
You'll feel a bit stronger every day."

"You'll soon have strong muscles
like me!" said Ronnie.
"Exercise helps to give us strong
muscles and bones. It gives
us energy too," said Mom.

Mia threw the ball and
        Pluto chased after it.
            "Energy like
            Pluto?"
            asked Mia.
            "Just like Pluto,"
            said Mom.

When they got home, Mia had a rest
while Mom and Ronnie made the beds.

"Making the beds is hard
work!" said Ronnie. "I can
feel my heart beating fast."
"Housework is good exercise.
It keeps you fit!" said Mom.

"Will it keep me fit for the
game?" said Ronnie.
Mom laughed. "It will help," she said.

Mia got up. "I'll sweep the floor," said Ronnie.
"Then I'll set the table. Come and help, Mia!"

"I'll help tomorrow,
when I'm better,"
said Mia.

At bedtime, Mia said,
"I'm too tired to
brush my teeth!"

"You'll get tooth decay!" joked Ronnie.
"You need to brush your teeth twice a day!"

Ronnie brushed his teeth carefully, rinsed his mouth with water, and smiled at the mirror. His teeth were white and strong.

"I don't want tooth decay!" said Mia. So she brushed her teeth and smiled at the mirror. Her teeth were white and strong too.

Mom put them to bed and kissed them both goodnight.

"I want to be in a basketball team like Ronnie," said Mia.

"I'll teach you to play tomorrow," said Ronnie.

The next day, they went to the park to practice. Mia was full of energy.

"Basketball is fun!" said Mia. "You'll have to train hard," said Ronnie. "And eat lots of healthy food!" said Mom.

"No problem!" grinned Mia. "I feel like I could join the team today!"

WRITE YOUR OWN STORY about keeping healthy. Make a chart like this to see if the things you do most days can help to keep you fit and healthy.

	Eating	Reading	Sleeping	Soccer	Washing
Gives me energy	✔				
Makes me strong	✔			✔	
Makes me think		✔			
Fights germs	✔		✔		✔
Gives me a rest			✔		

QUIZ

You think with your brain. What can you do to keep your brain **healthy**?

Answer on pages 4 and 5

Bones support your body. What helps to keep them strong?

Answer on pages 10 and 11

Germs can make you sick. What can you do to fight **germs**?

Answer on pages 20 and 21

What parts of your body do these things?

Pump blood around your body

Move your bones

Breathe

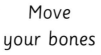

Chew

Answers on pages 8, 11, 12, 13

INDEX